Off Off Broadway Festival Plays

Thirty-Second Series

Selected by New York theatre critics, professionals, and the editorial staff of Samuel French, Inc. as the most important plays of the Thirty-Second Off Off Broadway Original Short Play Festival sponsored by Love Creek Productions.

OPENING
by Matthew Kelty

CIRCUIT BREAKERS
by Arthur W. French III

BRIGHT.APPLE.CRUSH.
by Steve Yockey

THE ROOSEVELT COUSINS, THOROUGHLY SAUCED
by Michael Lew

EVERY MAN
by Michael Niederman

THE GOOD BOOK
by Tiffany Antone

SAMUEL FRENCH

FOUNDED 1830

NEW YORK HOLLYWOOD LONDON TORONTO

SAMUELFRENCH.COM

IMPORTANT BILLING AND CREDIT
REQUIREMENTS

All producers of *OPENING, CIRCUIT BREAKERS, BRIGHT.APPLE. CRUSH., THE ROOSEVELT COUSINS, THOROUGHLY SAUCED, EVERY MAN,* and *THE GOOD BOOK must* give credit to the Author of the Play in all programs distributed in connection with performances of the Play, and in all instances in which the title of the Play appears for the purposes of advertising, publicizing or otherwise exploiting the Play and/or a production. The name of the Author *must* appear on a separate line on which no other name appears, immediately following the title and *must* appear in size of type not less than fifty percent of the size of the title type.

OPENING

(an imagined conversation inspired by true events)

by

MATTHEW KELTY

OPENING was presented by Urban Myth in June 2007 as part of Samuel French's Thirty-Second Annual Off Off Broadway Original Short Play Festival. The play was directed by Diana Basmajian. The cast was as follows:

DAVID O. SELZNICK . . . . .Michael Keller
HATTIE MCDANIEL . . . . Adrienne C. Moore

Many thanks to Theodore R. Clement, Pernell Walker, and Keisha Zollar, who helped develop this piece.

ABOUT THE AUTHOR

Matthew Kelty is a writer, actor, and director who lives in New York City. He studied with Romulus Linney and Jeffrey Sweet, and was awarded a Shubert Fellowship, while pursuing his MFA in Dramatic Writing. He has acted and directed regionally, Off Off, and Off Broadway; and his plays have been produced in Off Off and Off Broadway venues such as the DR2 Theatre, The Actors Studio, and The Theatre at Madison Square Garden. He is a member of The Dramatists Guild, and is proud to be one of the founders of Urban Myth.

CHARACTERS
(in order of appearance)

DAVID O. SELZNICK – Based on the historical figure. The producer of *Gone with the Wind*. A successful executive at MGM and RKO Studios, who went on to form Selznick International Pictures. His studio successes included *Anna Karenina*, *A Tale of Two Cities*, and *King Kong*. Successes as an independent producer included *A Star Is Born*, *The Adventures of Tom Sawyer* – and *Gone with the Wind*, which (adjusted for inflation) is still the highest-grossing film of all time.

HATTIE MCDANIEL – Based on the historical figure. Won an Academy Award for her role as Mammie in *Gone with the Wind*. A singer-songwriter; comedienne; and actress in radio, television, and film. The first African-American woman to sing on the radio, and the first African-American to win an Academy Award, she appeared in over 300 films (though she only received screen credit in about 80). Known in the African-American and entertainment communities for her generosity, elegance, and charm.

PLACE
Los Angeles, CA. The office of David O. Selznick.

TIME
November, 1939. One month before the world premiere of *Gone with the Wind* in Atlanta, GA.

COSTUME PLOT

Both characters should dress in clothes appropriate for a business meeting: a suit for David; and a slightly formal skirt, blouse, and jacket for Hattie (it would be great if she had gloves and a hat). It's important that the clothes are appropriate for the era of the play.

SET PLOT

The setting of the play is a Hollywood producer's office in 1939; it is more important that the "tone" of the set be right than that it be laid out in a specific way. A large desk faces the door through which Hattie will enter and David will leave, and the chair in which Hattie will sit; a small bar is off to the side. Ideally (with the right budget), the set would be lushly but tastefully appointed in the style of the time; but it is probably better to "suggest" the office with one or two appropriate pieces – or even to go abstract (cubes, etc.) – than to use pieces that are inappropriate for the time or for the setting.

PROPERTY PLOT

1930s-style intercom for David's desk
Several stacks of paper on David's desk
(If there is a bar:) Decanters and glasses

AUTHOR'S NOTE

Sometimes life provides us with a situation that is more complex and more ironic than any we could come up with as writers. Hattie McDaniel and David O. Selznick find themselves in a situation which perfectly encapsulates the times in which they lived, and represents the difficult decisions that artists (and all people) can be forced to make. It's impossible to know just what was said in the conversation portrayed here. But we know the circumstances that preceded and followed it; and we know that two individuals who considered themselves good, honest, independent people were faced with an excruciating choice. And as artists, we can imagine, empathize – and, hopefully, learn.

(Lights fade up. **DAVID O. SELZNICK** *sits behind a large desk in his studio office, rubbing his forehead with his fingertips. After a moment, he presses a button on his intercom.)*

SELZNICK. Sally, could you send Miss McDaniel in, please?

(A moment passes. **HATTIE McDANIEL** *enters the office, dressed for a business meeting. She waits for* **SELZNICK** *to speak.)*

SELZNICK *(cont'd).* Good morning, Hattie.

McDANIEL. Good morning, Mr. Selznick.

SELZNICK. Hattie. David. Please.

McDANIEL. Morning, David.

SELZNICK. How are you today?

McDANIEL. I'm fine.

SELZNICK. Good. Good. *(Small pause.)* I... Listen, Hattie, I just want to thank you again for your wonderful work on the film.

McDANIEL. Thank you, Mr. Selznick.

SELZNICK. David.

McDANIEL. Thank you, David.

SELZNICK. I mean, you're practically a co-star in the film – not really supporting at all.

McDANIEL. I'm glad you're pleased. Did you ask me to come in today so that you could thank me for my work?

SELZNICK. Yes.

McDANIEL. *(Turning to leave:)* Well, then...

SELZNICK. I mean, that wasn't the only reason, but yes, I... *(As* **McDANIEL** *turns back to him:)* I... Yes, I wanted to thank you. *(Small pause.)* You're wondering why we're here.

McDANIEL. I think I know, to tell the truth.

SELZNICK. You know.

McDANIEL. I think that I do.

    (Pause.)

SELZNICK. Well then for God's sake don't make me –

McDANIEL. I'm just hoping that I'm wrong.

SELZNICK. Hattie...

McDANIEL. *(Continuing:)* I mean, I'm praying that I'm wrong.

SELZNICK. This isn't something we can –

McDANIEL. Why am I here today, Mr. Selznick?

    (Pause.)

SELZNICK. I've been talking to one of our boys down in Atlanta. *(No response.)* There's been a problem with the programs for the premiere. *(No response.)* Some of the people – at the theatre and at the print house – they were unhappy with your picture. Unhappy that it was there. They didn't think it would be appropriate for you and Butterfly to be on the cover of the program.

McDANIEL. Are we inside the program?

SELZNICK. We're working on that. Certainly, you'll be on the programs in Los Angeles, New York... It's just in Atlanta.

    (Small pause.)

McDANIEL. Well, thank you for asking me. *(Turning to go:)* I don't know what Butterfly will say, but if you need to take my –

SELZNICK. Hattie, stop. **(McDANIEL** *turns back around.)* Please. Just let me finish. Let me say what I have to say. *(She stares at him and waits.)* We've been talking with the theatre, trying to determine where the cast will sit, where they'll enter. *(Small pause.)* They've told us that the theatre... It's segregated. The black actors won't be seated with the rest of the cast. You'll have to enter and exit separately, use separate restrooms – it's crazy, I know, it's ridiculous, but... The restaurant, too. The banquet before the premiere. They won't serve you. *(Small pause.)* You already know all of this.

McDANIEL. It's Hollywood, David. People talk.

(Small pause.)

SELZNICK. I don't want to see you treated badly, Hattie.

McDANIEL. Then don't let them treat me badly, David.

SELZNICK. I think it's just best for everyone involved if –

McDANIEL. Everyone?

SELZNICK. Yes, everyone, if you don't attend the premiere.

McDANIEL. How would that be better for me?

SELZNICK. Do you really want to be turned away at the door, Hattie? With all the press there watching? That's embarrassing for us, humiliating for you –

McDANIEL. They wouldn't do it. Not with people taking pictures.

SELZNICK. They're already making us change the program.

McDANIEL. You could tell them, just tell them. They'd let me in.

SELZNICK. And the public would stream out the doors, while the cameras snapped. We've sunk a lot of money into this movie; we can't have people running out of the premiere. It'll be in every paper in the country.

(Pause.)

McDANIEL. *(With mock sincerity:)* Maybe I could go, and then leave once we get to the theatre.

SELZNICK. I don't see that that's going to –

McDANIEL. *(Continuing, over* SELZNICK, *allowing the sarcasm to show:)* You know, just so Vivienne can have someone to carry her things. I've got a really nice kerchief I could wrap around my head that's not too worn ...

SELZNICK. Hattie, I don't know what else to do.

McDANIEL. Move the premiere. Why does Atlanta get to have the premiere if they're going to treat your actors so badly?

SELZNICK. Half the movie takes place in Atlanta.

McDANIEL. Half *The Wizard of Oz* takes place over the rainbow, but they didn't put little Judy Garland in a hot air balloon and send her –

SELZNICK. We can't move the premiere. We've already announced it, gotten so far along in the planning. If we move it, it'll be a scandal.

McDANIEL. And it won't be a scandal if your black actors don't go to the premiere?

(Small pause.)

SELZNICK. Not to as many people, no.

(Pause.)

McDANIEL. Well, I guess I didn't know why you called me in here after all. I thought you wanted to talk about how to handle Atlanta, but instead you just called me in to give me an order about –

SELZNICK. Well, the publicity boys actually think we've come up with something that ... *(Small pause.)* You know that I appreciate the ... It's a wonderful performance you gave us in this movie, Hattie.

McDANIEL. You said that earlier, yes.

SELZNICK. It's really very fine.

McDANIEL. Thank you.

SELZNICK. I think it's deserving of recognition. From the Academy. I'd like to recommend you for consideration for Best Supporting Actress after we open.

(Small pause.)

McDANIEL. Thank you, Mr. Selznick.

SELZNICK. David, please.

McDANIEL. David.

SELZNICK. Hattie. I'd like for you to write me a letter.

McDANIEL. About the nomination? I didn't know you needed a –

SELZNICK. I'd like for you to write me a letter saying that you have a previous commitment, and won't be able to attend the premiere in Atlanta.

McDANIEL. And the one is dependent on the other?

SELZNICK. I've really tried to work with you on this movie, Hattie.

McDANIEL. Oh?

SELZNICK. You wanted us to take "nigger" out of the script, we took it out.

McDANIEL. And left in "darkies." You wanted to leave in "nigger."

SELZNICK. It's a historical document, Hattie.

McDANIEL. It's a movie.

SELZNICK. Still, you wanted it out, and I took it out.

McDANIEL. And you did that just for me? That's so sweet, David. It didn't have anything to do with Butterfly and Oscar coming to you and –

SELZNICK. You sent them over.

McDANIEL. *(Continuing:)* – or the Hayes Commission or the editorials in the Negro papers protesting you even turning this book into a –

SELZNICK. I am trying to give you a way out of this. Trying to find a graceful way for us to handle this. The premiere is in Atlanta. The theater is segregated. We want to avoid a scandal. If you would just write me a letter saying that you have prior commitments, then –

McDANIEL. Then they win.

SELZNICK. Yes. Yes, they do win. You're right. And I hate to see it. But maybe you win, Hattie, in just a few months. Maybe they win that night, but you win at the Awards in the Spring. The first Negro to win an Academy Award, Hattie. Wouldn't that be something?

McDANIEL. You keep bringing those things up together.

SELZNICK. You said it yourself, Hattie. This is Hollywood. People talk.

McDANIEL. Talk about what?

SELZNICK. All kinds of things besides someone's performance. Like whether they're a team player, whether people would want to work with them again. A good role, that's only half of it. Maybe less.

McDANIEL. You're saying I won't win if I make a fuss about this.

SELZNICK. I'm saying you won't work again.

(Small pause.)

McDANIEL. I think that's a little extreme. *(Small pause.)* You'd ruin my career because I won't write you a letter.

SELZNICK. There are plenty of colored actors in this town who want to work.

McDANIEL. And not enough roles as slaves and mammies to go around.

SELZNICK. What's that quote you gave in that interview, Hattie? Something... "I've worked as a maid in real life... The money's better in Hollywood." Something.

McDANIEL. I said I'd rather play a maid than work as one.

SELZNICK. Words to live by. *(Small pause.)* It's going to get better, Hattie. It'll just take some time. Make sure you're around for when it gets better.

*(**McDANIEL** doesn't answer. **SELZNICK** turns to a stack of papers on his desk and begins to shuffle through them.)*

SELZNICK *(cont'd)*. Good, good, terrific. Now, I'm going to call one of the boys in from publicity to work with you on the letter. We'll keep it nice and simple, short, nothing we could get caught –

McDANIEL. But David, what if we –

*(**SELZNICK** throws his papers onto the desk in frustration; they scatter all over the desk and the floor.)*

SELZNICK. All right, I've had enough. I'm going to get someone to work with you on this. I'll be back in five minutes. If you're here, you're going to have a signed letter on my desk before you go home. If you're not here, don't bother coming back. Do you understand?

(He gets up and leaves without waiting for an answer. **McDANIEL** *looks around the office for several moments. Some of the paper has fallen at her feet; she picks it up and puts it on the desk. She looks around some more, then picks up some of the other papers that have fallen. As she places them on the desk, her voice is heard reading the text of* **McDANIEL**'s *letter to* **SELZNICK.** *The voice continues as she straightens the papers on the desk, and then possibly begins to straighten the office a little. She cleans as the voice continues and the lights begin to fade.)*

McDANIEL'S VOICE. Dear Mr. Selznick: Thank you so much for your invitation to attend the world premiere of the studio's new film, *Gone with the Wind,* in Atlanta next month. I am thrilled to be a part of the film, and hope that the premiere goes well. Unfortunately, I will be unable to attend the premiere, due to circumstances that I'm unable to change. Best of luck in Atlanta. Please accept my apologies. And my deep, deep regrets.

(Lights out.)

END

CIRCUIT BREAKERS

by

ARTHUR W. FRENCH III

CIRCUIT BREAKERS was developed and produced by the RCL Writer's Workshop, Le Wilhelm and Kathy Towson, producers. The play was originally done as part of RCL's Brief Acts Series in March 2007 with the cast was as follows:

DANNY . . . . Hank Dennis

THERESA . . . . Candice Myers

JORDAN . . . . Norma Nongauza

CARMEN . . . . \ . . . . Monica Kedzie Romero

CIRCUIT BREAKERS was performed in June 2007 as part of the Thirty-Second Samuel French, Inc. Annual Off Off Broadway Original Short Play Festival. The production was produced by RCL Writer's Workshop with Le Wilhelm and Kathy Towson. The cast was as follows:

DANNY . . . . Hank Dennis

THERESA . . . . Candice Myers

JORDAN . . . . Norma Nongauza

CARMEN . . . . Staxx Cordero

ABOUT THE AUTHOR

Arthur W. French III has been writing plays since he was a teenager. His first play, *Teens Today*, was first performed at Maxwell Glanville's American Community Theatre. It went from there to be a finalist at the NYC Young Playwright's Festival. Mr. French's play *Workday*, directed by his father Arthur French, was in the Samuel French Off Off Broadway Short Play Festival, *Chad and Rose*, was in the 2005 Samuel French Festival, and *Shutter Speeds* was a finalist in the 2006 Samuel French Festival. Mr. French was studied playwrighting under Steve Carter, Leslie Lee and Henry Miller. Mr. French is a Member of the RCL Writer's Workshop, and the Martha J. Thomas Writer's Workshop. Mr. French would like to thank his family, friends, all actors, and writers for their support.

Circuit Breakers is about a guy who thinks he's found the perfect mate, only to find out that takes work.

CAST OF CHARACTERS

All characters are in their mid-20's - early 30's
DANNY - Regular guy
THERESA - Girl-next-door type
JORDAN - Sexy, confident
CARMEN - Vampish, direct

SET

In the middle of the stage should be a sofa. In front of the sofa is a coffee table. On the coffee table lies a remote control. Perhaps there is a small table stage right.

PROPS

2 remote controls (1 for Danny, 1 for Carmen)
1 plate
1 grilled cheese sandwich
1 contract

COSTUMES

DANNY - Regular shirt and slacks
THERESA - Blouse, mini skirt
JORDAN - Sexy dress
CARMEN - Miniskirt, heels, trench coat

(**Scene:** *An apartment in Queens. In the apartment are* **DANNY** *and* **THERESA**. *They are cuddling together watching TV.*)

DANNY. Boy, they don't make those movies like they used to.

THERESA. Yeah. I certainly love those romance movies. They put me in the mood.

DANNY. Well, are you in the mood?

THERESA. I am, whenever you are.

(Both kiss.)

DANNY. Theresa, this is a milestone for me.

THERESA. Really?

DANNY. For me at least. I've been going out with the same lady for three months and I feel so comfortable with you.

THERESA. I feel the same way. It's like our modems met.

DANNY. I love your computer terminology. I'm thinking about taking the next step.

THERESA. And that is.

DANNY. Renewing you.

THERESA. Renewing me?

DANNY. Yeah!

THERESA. For how long?

DANNY. Another three months.

THERESA. Is that it?

DANNY. What do you mean?

THERESA. Well, we've been together three months, and you have said it's been the best three months, am I right?

DANNY. Yes.

THERESA. And that, we are compatible, right?

DANNY. Right.

THERESA. So why not renew me permanently?

DANNY. I want to be sure.

THERESA. I don't know what's to decide.

DANNY. Theresa

THERESA. I mean you created me.

DANNY. I did.

THERESA. I was tailor made for you, the Theresa T1250, right? I was programmed to the letter to satisfy every need, your intellect, your soul, your needs, your desires.

DANNY. You have, but I'm thinking more on the line of a trial period.

THERESA. You've had ninety days.

DANNY. I don't need to hear this.

(**DANNY** *reaches for a device, and tries to turn her off.*)

DANNY. Why won't you turn off.

THERESA. Usually after ninety days, the remote doesn't work. Any T1250's that hit ninety-days we all go from the remote to the main terminal. You obviously didn't read your manual.

DANNY. Theresa, just stop. I command you to stop.

THERESA. Not until we talk about this.

DANNY. There's nothing to say.

THERESA. How can you say that? You committed to me, you programmed me, and now your not sure. Look at me Danny, really look at me. You programmed my body, my curves, my kissing, my lusts, what have I done for you not to commit to me? *(pause)* Is there someone else? Is it that T1590 with the fake breasts?

DANNY. All of you is fake.

THERESA. True, but hers are injected with the elastic skin implants. Cheap imitation. *(pause)* There's someone else. I can sense it. I know your instincts, Danny. I know every positive, and every negative vibe you give.

DANNY. I've been thinking about this girl.

THERESA. And.

DANNY. And well.

THERESA. Well, what?

DANNY. She's umm....

THERESA. Stammering as usual.

DANNY. She's human!

(**THERESA** *is stunned.*)

THERESA. Human?

DANNY. Yeah.

THERESA. Oh god, Danny! A human?

DANNY. She's an employee at where I work.

THERESA. I need a drink. I need a recharge.

(*She pulls out, a wire, and charges herself to the modem.*)

THERESA. Oh, that feels good.

DANNY. Theresa, I may have a call coming in.

THERESA. It can wait.

(**THERESA** *pulls the wire out.*)

THERESA. Okay, now I'm better.

DANNY. I hope you didn't cross your wires again.

THERESA. Why do you care, Mister? Go back to human beings.

DANNY. I just went out with her, Theresa, a few times, and we hit it off.

THERESA. You can't hit it off with me? Didn't we have fun?

DANNY. Yes.

THERESA. Didn't my excitement please you?

DANNY. Yes.

THERESA. Where does that leave me? I'm supposed to sit here like a... like a mistress.

DANNY. I didn't say that.

THERESA. But that's what you inferred.

DANNY. Not at all.

THERESA. Well, what do you call it?

DANNY. Theresa, you're perfect, but your not....

THERESA. Not what?

DANNY. Real. I need to feel something, something that's there. I want to be with a woman who's human. You're a great person.

THERESA. Oh, I'm a person now? Wow, thanks for noting the difference.

DANNY. That's not what I meant. She has a great personality! She makes me laugh

THERESA. You can program me to be funny. I can laugh at your jokes. I'm a great kiss ass. For only twenty dollars, you can add submissive command to the control switch.

DANNY. That's just it, I can always turn you on and off. With Jordan, I don't have to. She's real. We can love, cuddle.

THERESA. In other words, a bimbo.

(There is a knock on the door.)

DANNY. And, she's here.

THERESA. What?

DANNY. She's picking me up. We're going out to the movies, and then some dinner.

THERESA. And I made your favorite tonight. Grilled cheese. Your flaunting her in front of me, great move!

DANNY. Don't burn your circuits up.

THERESA. I'm already into overdrive, Danny, don't push it.

*(**DANNY** goes to the door. In enters **JORDAN**. She is in a mini-dress.)*

JORDAN. Hey baby!

DANNY. Sweet heart!

*(Both kiss. **THERESA** starts tapping her foot. She coughs.)*

THERESA. I'm Theresa. Danny's compatible mate! You must be Jordan.

JORDAN. I am. How are you?

THERESA. Fine, just fine.

JORDAN. I've heard all about you.

THERESA. That's funny. I've just heard all about you.

DANNY. Theresa, Could you just cool down? Recharge again?

JORDAN. I totally understand, baby. These T1250's are sensitive, don't they short out once in a while?

DANNY. No, Theresa's pretty durable!

THERESA. Yeah, they added a booster microchip, so that in any moment of pleasure and passion, we can give an extra boost to that mode. Can you?

JORDAN. Every step of the way.

DANNY. Can we all sit down?

JORDAN. Danny, shouldn't we hit the movie?

DANNY. We got time. Anyway, this is some foreign film.

JORDAN. *Les pommes frites* is supposed to be fabulous.

DANNY. I can see a commercial about French fries anytime.

JORDAN. It's the weay Bucco films it. Like a hardcore concert at CBGB's.

DANNY. Anything for you, Jordan!

JORDAN. Tres bon!

THERESA. Would madame real person like something to drink? Water? Soda?

JORDAN. No thanks!

THERESA. I'll bring your meal.

(THERESA *exits.*)

DANNY. I'm sorry about Theresa. She's taking this hard.

JORDAN. I would too, if you were leaving me for a real person. Especially if you created her.

DANNY. They really did a good job with her. I mean the company got everything. They got everything. They got every nuance of what I was looking for.

JORDAN. And you hated it.

DANNY. I thought I would like perfection.

JORDAN. You wanted excitement, wildness, spontaneity, let-it-all-hang-out-ness.

DANNY. I guess that's where you came in.

JORDAN. I sensed that in you.

DANNY. And I love dancing close to you. Just to hear a real heartbeat.

JORDAN. And I've got a big heart.

DANNY. Yes, you do.

JORDAN. I hope I'm not a rebound thing.

DANNY. What?

JORDAN. That your only with me, because your bored being with an appliance.

DANNY. Theresa's not an appliance, she's…she's….

JORDAN. Artificial. I'm not!

*(They both laugh. **THERESA** enters angrily. She puts the grilled cheese sandwich on **DANNY**'s lap.)*

DANNY. Theresa!

THERESA. Your grilled cheese sir!

JORDAN. Is there a lock and remote to hold her down?

THERESA. The server is on now, so I can fly off the handle, and have any emotions that hit me at any time.

DANNY. Theresa, could you please chill out?

THERESA. For you, I'll do it. Because I love you.

*(**THERESA** takes his hand. **DANNY** gently rebuffs it. She is hurt. He picks up the sandwich, and eats.)*

DANNY. The grilled cheese is great, Theresa. Perfect as always.

*(**THERESA** nods "yes")*

DANNY. Jordan, take a bite.

JORDAN. No, I'm not hungry.

DANNY. Come on! Just a little taste. She puts a hint of parmesan on it. It's real good.

JORDAN. I'm on a diet, baby, you know that.

DANNY. You must be a bulimic or something, because you look fabulous!

THERESA. You know I would eat something, Jordan, but I can't eat. I can keep up this physical beauty for all eternity. Can you say that?

JORDAN. I can bleed.

THERESA. Low blow, Jordan. I can make you bleed.

JORDAN. Danny, I think we should go now.

DANNY. I hear you. No violence here!

THERESA. You think your better than me, that you can't my dish?

JORDAN. I don't need to eat anything.

THERESA. Because you can't eat.

DANNY. What are you talking about?

THERESA. She's a robot too.

DANNY. This is above and beyond crazy.

JORDAN. I've had enough of this.

THERESA. I'm telling you, she is. Androids can't eat anything. They've put a denial chip in her and everything.

DANNY. There's a conspiracy chip in your head.

THERESA. I know. You created me.

DANNY. Good bye Theresa. Don't wait up for me.

THERESA. She obviously doesn't love you.

(**DANNY** *and* **JORDAN** *stop.*)

THERESA. If I was able to eat, and my boyfriend slaved to make a sandwich for me, and he asked me to take a taste, I would, because I love him.

JORDAN. I don't need some oversized, fake tin-woman to tell me how I should be with my man.

THERESA. Your chicken.

DANNY. Jordan, come on, let's go.

JORDAN. No, I'm going to prove a point right now, just to shut her up.

DANNY. Jordan, geeze.

(*JORDAN goes over, takes a bite of the sandwich, eats it, and swallows.*)

JORDAN. Satisfied?

THERESA. Yeah.

JORDAN (*smirking*) Good. Lets g-g-g-g-go.

(*All of a sudden* **JORDAN** *starts to twitch as though she's shorting out.*)

DANNY. Jordan, you okay?

JORDAN. I'm fine. Let's go. I'm (*speech starts to slow down*) ready to go to the sh-sh-show. What's happening to me?

THERESA. She's shorting out. She's a T2560.

DANNY. What?

THERESA. The T2560 is much more sophisticated than me. She has all the human qualities that I have, the only difference is this robot can digest, however this isn't the perfected model.

JORDAN (*Slowing down*) This is crazy. I can't be a robot!

THERESA. Unfortunately, Jordan, you are. The grilled cheese is shorting out your vital circuits, and fuses that make you tick. Your going to shut down soon forever, say your final words quick.

DANNY. Jordan.

JORDAN I guess this cancels dinner plans.

DANNY. This is no time for jokes, baby.

JORDAN (*slow motion*) Danny, I just want to let you know your a great guy and I've enjoyed the time I've spent with you. This really sucks! I want you to know that.... that. I love you!

(*She freezes like a statue.* **THERESA** *is smug.*)

DANNY. You knew about this?

THERESA. No, I didn't. I suspected. But now that you know.

DANNY. How could I have not known.

THERESA. You probably have a fetish for androids. Android-maniacus.

DANNY. You're enjoying this.

THERESA. Face it Danny, your not capable of loving real people. That's just a fact, you can only deal with the things you create. The sooner you understand that, the sooner you can move on.

DANNY. Must you be so honest?

THERESA. You programmed me to be. Oh, Danny, here we go again with your sulking mode. Get over it.

(*DANNY reaches for the remote.*)

DANNY. 777-9311

(*All of a sudden THERESA starts to short.*)

THERESA. Danny, what are you doing?

DANNY. I found the failsafe!

THERESA. (*shorting*) Danny, d-d-d-don't do this. (*speech slowing down*) I was looking out for your best interest.

DANNY. And I'm now looking out for mine. Goodbye Theresa!

THERESA. I …I….I…Love you.

(*She freezes like a rag doll. DANNY smugly looks at her. Goes back to his sofa, and starts to eat the rest of his sandwich.*)

DANNY. Oh well. Perfect as always.

(*There is a knock at the door.*)

DANNY. Come in, the door's open.

(**CARMEN** *enters. She is in a trench coat.*)

CARMEN. Hi Danny.

DANNY. And you are?

CARMEN. I was summoned here. The failsafe went off.

DANNY. From what?

(**CARMEN** *walks over to* **JORDAN.**)

CARMEN. Ahh, the robot junkyard.

(**CARMEN** *pulls out a remote, and programs it.*)

CARMEN. T2750. Not all the kinks were pulled out, Windows Millenium version. Okay.

(*She presses the button.* **JORDAN**'s *arm moves sporadically, She tries to talk, but garbles her words.*)

CARMEN. Food has totally messed up for circuits. She'll be headed for the scrap heap. Nice job. Cute face, interesting build.

(**CARMEN** *walks over to* **THERESA**.)

CARMEN. Custom made one! Ahh, I can tell! Let me check her.

(**CARMEN** *programs* **THERESA**. *Her arms move. She moves in a robotic way, and then stops.*)

CARMEN. She's working. Oh, got sick of her? 90 days lapsed. Smart guy! Found the failsafe! Poor thing. She cared too much.

DANNY. Excuse me, Miss. Do I know you?

CARMEN. You should. You created me.

DANNY. When was this?

CARMEN. When you walked into the robot factory. I was the first prototype, but you threw me to the side. I'm Carmen? Come on now! I'm your fantasy robot.

(*She takes off her trench coat, and is in a revealing dress.*)

CARMEN. I was a mix of your ex-girlfriend, first and third high-school crush, and the girl you had a thing for, but you kept picking up the phone and hanging up on?

DANNY. Oh, yeah.

CARMEN. You had wanted a more mellow model, because you felt I was too fast for you, but that was the old Carmen. I'm the new-and-improved Carmen Z28. I'm not a demo model, so I can show you live what's up. As you can see, my body was created via your pictures, and fantasy re-creation. As you see my shoulders, legs, were custom made. If you watch closely.

(**CARMEN** *sits down on the sofa.*)

CARMEN. I can cross my legs very slowly, and seductively, or quick and innocently. I can be tailor made to fit your every needs. Come and sit down.

(**DANNY** *sits down on the sofa.*)

CARMEN. With the touch of my hand, as I will do here....

(**DANNY** *all of a sudden is in ecstasy.*)

CARMEN. ...I can find your pleasure spot. I knew these two couldn't. And watch this.

(**CARMEN** *points toward the CD player. Romantic music starts playing.*)

CARMEN. Music to lighten the mood by R. Kelly or Luther or whatever gets your libido working. And since these two are down for the night, I'm here to settle you down.

DANNY. Okay!

CARMEN. Another thing about me that you'll like is that my emotions are intact, unlike these two tin machines. My program is on even keel. They didn't make a mistake in me. Can't you tell?

DANNY. No, not at all.

CARMEN. I knew you can see the difference. And since I'm on your mind, because you created me, I have a contract here for you to sign on the dotted line.

(**CARMEN** *pulls out the contract and hands it to* **DANNY.**)

DANNY. For what?

CARMEN. A little formality, unlike Miss 90 days there, and Miss Hungry Girl. I am covered for a year, and you don't have to worry about breakdowns, recharges, any of that stuff.

DANNY. Well, I'd like to take my time.

CARMEN. What's the big thinking for? If it didn't work out with these two, you know it will with me? Why delay?

DANNY. Because I'm not sure.

*(**CARMEN** turns off the CD player.)*

CARMEN. Then obviously you don't know yourself. You obviously don't know what you want.

DANNY. If I asked you to do something, you can do anything right?

CARMEN. Anything baby that you want and desire, I can.

DANNY. Okay, can you make a grilled cheese sandwich?

CARMEN. *(laughs)* Honey, I'm not programmed to cook.

DANNY. Then I've made my decision.

CARMEN. And a great choice you made sweetness!

*(**DANNY** takes the remote, and clicks it. **CARMEN** starts to short.)*

CARMEN. Your shutting me down?

DANNY. You got it beautiful.

CARMEN. You must have some serious issues to shut me down. I'm the best choice.

DANNY. Buh bye, Carmen.

CARMEN. At least I look hot ! I... love... me!

*(**CARMEN** freezes. **DANNY** looks at all of them. He puts the remote down, goes over to the phone And dials it.)*

DANNY. Hello. Eliot Tech Support? Yes, hi. Do you think you can send me a robot that just knows how to cook a grilled cheese sandwich?

(The lights fade.)

END OF PLAY

BRIGHT. APPLE. CRUSH.

by

STEVE YOCKEY

BRIGHT.APPLE.CRUSH. had its New York premiere at Vital Theatre Company, New York City, with Stephen Sunderlin as the artistic director and Linda Ames Key as the producing director. it premiered as part of Vital Signs: New Works Festival, 2006. The production was directed by Bob Cline. The cast was as follows:

ETHAN . . . . Chris Van Hoy

NANCY . . . . Mary Ann Welshans

DAN . . . . Michael Busillo

CHARACTERS

ETHAN – A man, early twenties, charismatic, loose. He has cigarettes, a lighter and an easy calmness about him.

NANCY – A woman, early twenties, put together. She has an apple but guards it from the audience.

DAN – A man, early twenties, quiet, nervous, sweet. He is dressed stylishly and wears a pair of heavy boots. He has a somewhat-healed black eye.

NOTES

[ ] indicates overlapping dialogue.

In the overlapping monologues, key moments should rise to prominence. An ebb and flow of the stories.

The piece moves as swiftly as possible without glossing over details.

SET

Three pools of light spaced evenly across the stage.

PROPS

A pack of cigarettes
A lighter
An apple
A pair of boots

If smoking on stage (even limited) is not an available option, Ethan can repeatedly light a cigarette and put it out without taking a drag. Or simply play with a cigarette lighter.

(Light rises to dim, revealing three people standing on stage.)

(Lights up full on **ETHAN**. *He is lighting a cigarette. Takes a single drag and immediately puts it out with a smirk.)*

ETHAN. It's not going to help.

(Lights up full on **NANCY**. *She is polishing a red apple. She looks up and hides it behind her back.)*

NANCY. Teaching is not for everyone.

(Lights up full on **DAN**. *He is tying up his left boot. He finishes and stands.)*

DAN. Love can make you, I don't know, so you don't think straight.

ETHAN. I should introduce myself. Ethan.

NANCY. I'm Nancy. Nancy Miller. You might have read about me...

DAN. My name's Dan.

ETHAN. And I mean I can explain it, absolutely, but it'll only make things [worse.]

NANCY. [Those kids] were horrible. I can't say a single nice thing. And their parents [were just...]

DAN. [I never] could put it into words.

NANCY. Some people shouldn't be allowed to have children.

DAN. He was the best thing that ever happened to me.

NANCY. There was one little boy who would kick me as hard as he could. Every chance he got. [I couldn't believe it.]

DAN. [I couldn't believe it] when he asked me out. It was like, like...

NANCY. Ridiculously painful. Every day, every time, kicking me. And he was one of the better kids. If that gives you an idea of how bad they really were.

ETHAN. But really, I think if you could have seen the fire. I mean, it might not be your thing, but it was seriously impressive. Seriously. Just an amazing fire. Big and hot, waves of heat, so you couldn't look right at it. You had to look away.

DAN. He is, was the absolute love of my life.

ETHAN. I didn't look away though.

NANCY. It's hard when you decide you're really going to try and help people. Become a teacher; take a job where you can make a difference. Where you think you can make a difference. It's hard when that turns out to be impossible.

DAN. After months of dating, the best kind of dating, the sweet, hot, can't be without them kind of dating, we decided to move in together.

ETHAN. *(He lights another cigarette while speaking and then puts it out again quickly after one drag…)* So like I said, I can explain it. She was cheating on me. That afternoon, there was some kind of accident at the local school and they sent everyone home, I mean I usually work most of the night. So I came home early.

DAN. Big decision: to live together. But it felt right.

ETHAN. He was there, in my bed, with my wife, just crazy sex. So they didn't even, I walked in, but they didn't see me. I stood there for a while and they still didn't see me. Because they were so into… So I turned around and walked out.

DAN. It wasn't perfect dating, I don't want to sound, you know, it was good. We did have some fights, no big deal. Some of them had even become kind of physical, but it was nothing.

NANCY. That's frustrating. Especially when you can help a kid and they don't want it. Like they know anything. When you're trying to help a kid and they act like they're smarter than you.

DAN. So I asked him to move in and he said yes.

NANCY. A bunch of fucking ten year olds.

ETHAN. I didn't know the guy. I thought maybe I would know him.

NANCY. Like they know anything… except how to me mean. No one warns you about that, in college, in your classes. Even when you're assistant teaching, no one tells you. Kids can be terrible.

DAN. The second night after he moved in, I spilled a bottle of wine. It was just careless.

ETHAN. There was rope in the closet at the end of the hall. I could still hear them.

DAN. He hit me so hard that I blacked out, square in the jaw. Just a sharp pain and then nothing. When I woke up, he was asleep. I wasn't even sure it even… And then I cleaned up the wine.

NANCY. I remember so vividly the moment when I just snapped.

DAN. That started to happen a lot. Not the spilling…

NANCY. I was at my desk.

DAN. The hitting.

NANCY. I was trying to explain photosynthesis. Well, the way you explain photosynthesis to a bunch of ten year olds.
(In her condescending teacher's voice…)
"The plants have their leaves and the sunlight shines down, [bright light…"]

DAN. [Bright light] shining in through the curtains. My apartment faced these security lights. It never really got dark. And he hadn't noticed until he moved in, so this became another source of tension. Something that was my fault.

NANCY. And as I'm trying to teach these kids something, I'm writing on the board, with my back to them like this…
(She turns and speaks over her shoulder.)

And I get hit with something, hit hard in the shoulder and then again in the leg. And again in the hip.

DAN. It got so the bruises were becoming something I had to explain. I felt like a bad after school special. But then, it seemed like most of the stuff actually could have been avoided, if I had just paid more attention.

NANCY. It took me a moment to even realize what was happening. They were throwing rocks at me. These kids in my class, these young kids, were actually throwing rocks at me. [And laughing.]

ETHAN. [And laughing,] they were laughing and grunting and all of the sudden it sounded like I was in a tunnel, with traffic, this roaring white noise that kind of shoved everything else into the background. And I realized I was squeezing the rope so tight that my hands were raw.

DAN. And that was okay for a while. He was the first person I ever loved, he was the first guy I ever had sex with, and really good sex. He was everything. And you take the good with the bad. That's how it works.

NANCY. I couldn't even speak.

ETHAN. *(He lights another cigarette, takes a single drag, looks at it while speaking and then puts out the cigarette.)* They were still having sex when I hit the guy in the back of the head. I don't even remember really what I hit him with. It was heavy. She screamed out, but it was muddled by the noise in my ears. After I hit her a couple of times, she stopped moving.

DAN. Eventually I got to the point where I stopped flinching. Didn't even try to avoid it. And he seemed to understand. I just accepted it…

NANCY. They were hitting [me.]

DAN. [While] he was hitting [me.]

ETHAN. [Eventually] I stopped hitting them. And tied them to the bed.

NANCY. I took the rest of the day off. I went [home.]

DAN. [And] then last night something was [different.]

ETHAN. [And] I walked [downstairs.]

DAN. [And] I didn't feel anything at all when he hit [me.]

ETHAN. [And] I walked [outside.]

DAN. [And] I didn't fall [down.]

ETHAN. [And] I walked to the [garage.]

DAN. [And] I was aware on some level that my body was moving, but it was like watching a movie, you know? But standing right up against the screen, so the images don't make sense.

NANCY. *(She pulls the apple from behind her back where she has been hiding it in one hand or the other...)* While I was at home, I had some time to think. To really think about what happened, about everything that had happened in my three months at that schools. I made some decisions. About those fucking ten years olds.

(**ETHAN** *lights a cigarette, looks at it, puts it out without taking a drag.*)

If you can't teach them to even be human, then what good are they?

DAN. It's all kind of a blur still.

ETHAN. The garage is where we kept the gasoline.

NANCY. *(She handles the apple.)* And then it was clear. And really [simple...]

ETHAN. [It was] really [simple.]

DAN. [It seemed] so... simple. I just, I looked down and somehow he was on the floor. And there was blood. And I kept bring my boot down on his neck and face. I remember thinking that it shouldn't be happening, but not having any control over it. There was a point where I didn't even recognize him anymore and my boot was covered in blood.

(*He looks at his boot.*)

NANCY. *(She tosses and catches the apple.)* The healthiest snack in the world.

ETHAN. *(He lights the lighter once or twice.)* I always carry a lighter.

DAN. All of the sudden I could hear my breathing and my heart slamming in my chest, tears on my face, wet and sticky. But I still didn't stop.

ETHAN. Just like this…

(He lights a cigarette, takes a single drag, holds out his lighter, lights it and leans forward as if setting something on fire. He then backs away, exhaling the smoke while saying…)

And whoosh!

NANCY. I passed them out and said: *(A return to the teacher's voice…)* "All right, it's important that you all stay healthy. But I know not everyone loves to eat apples. So here's a little deal for you guys: Whoever finishes their apple first will get an extra 20 minutes at recess."

DAN. It all happened [so quickly.]

ETHAN. [It all happened] [so quickly.]

NANCY. [It all happened] so quickly. They just started tearing into the apples. And I'll confess that [it was exciting.]

DAN. [It was exciting] and horrifying all at once. [It was a rush.]

ETHAN. [It was a rush] of flame up the side of the building. Faster than I would have imagined.

NANCY. I didn't expect them all to react with such enthusiasm for just 20 extra minutes at recess. I thought it would somehow be harder.

DAN. I finally stopped.

NANCY. I might have used too much poison.

ETHAN. I'm sure they woke up at some point.

NANCY. If I had known they'd be so voracious, I probably would have eased off a bit.

DAN. I was covered in blood.

NANCY. I like to think I would have been more restrained.

ETHAN. I like to think they woke up, right in the middle of it.

DAN. You never think of yourself as…

NANCY. But that might be too generous really.

DAN. When it was over, I didn't really know what to do. I took off my boots; I didn't want to be in them. I didn't think, I don't, I just took them off. And he was laying there kind of moving some, so I took my clothes off, [put them in the washing machine and went, naked, back into the living room. He was still moving. I picked up my boots and took them to the bathtub. I let it fill up while I sat in the tub scrubbing the boots. After just a few minutes, the water was red and soapy, but the boots were clean. Wet and clean. I drained the tub, took a shower, cleaned it with bleach. I dried myself off, moved my clothes from the washer to the dryer, threw in the boots and walked back into the living room. He was still moving a little, breathing through, trying to breath. I watched him while I waited for the dryer to finish. At one point he reached towards me and I started to sob uncontrollably. When my clothes were dry, I got dressed again, even the boots. And I called the police and asked for an ambulance.]

NANCY. [It took about 10 minutes before the first one started convulsing. But it happened quickly after that. I wouldn't let any of them go to the bathroom, I wouldn't let any of them leave. I told them to stay in their seats and for the first time, and I don't know if they were afraid or disoriented or just stunned, but they did as they were told. [[I sat behind my desk and watched these horrible children drop to the floor or collapse onto their own desks one by one in pools of spit and some crimson streaks. And they were crying and asking for help and confused. Clearly confused. It's hard for me to say this, but honestly it was a real delight to see these worthless children suffer the way that I had suffered when all I wanted to do was help them become better people. There were only one or two left mildly conscious when I even began to realize that this might cause a problem.]]]

ETHAN. [[I watched the fire, stood really close to it. I watched it for a while. When the roof caved in, this billow of smoke was released all at once; this thick, dark smoke and I had to move back a good bit because I was coughing so much. I didn't really think of anything, but I got in my car to drive away. And I couldn't, I couldn't make myself leave. Instead I just backed up and kept watching the house the burn. I needed to watch it for as long as I could. When I heard the sirens from the fire trucks, then I drove away.]]

*(Pause. **NANCY** takes a bite of the apple. The other two men look at her as she chews and swallows. They all look out again…)*

NANCY. I knew they wouldn't understand. No one. So the general reaction didn't surprise me. Maybe some of the other teachers, but no, no one did.

DAN. I feel like I could hear the sirens for hours before anyone actually got there. I just stayed the couch, far away from him.

NANCY. But I think the other teachers were secretly proud of me.

DAN. It took forever, but I could hear the sirens. They said, they told me that there was a huge fire a few blocks down. Those were the sirens. That they were sorry it took so long for the ambulance to…

ETHAN. When they spoke to me, the police told me that they had assumed I was the man in bed with my wife.

DAN. I told them I came home from drinks with friends and found him like that.

ETHAN. So they were surprised.

NANCY. I don't even read the papers or watch television anymore, because of the ridiculous things people are saying about me.

DAN. I rode with him in the ambulance to the hospital, I held his hand, and waited while he was in surgery.

ETHAN. There's going to be an investigation. I suppose that makes sense.

NANCY. Saying I hate children. It's amazing what people will believe.

DAN. I don't know what I'll do when he wakes up. When he can tell people what happened. What I, what I did… to him.

ETHAN. I didn't really try cover anything up. I wasn't thinking that way I guess. I wasn't thinking [at all…]

NANCY. [Listen,] I took that job because I love kids.

ETHAN. And I'm still sure they deserved it. I feel it in my bones.

NANCY. Those weren't kids though, you see? They were… something else.

DAN. I sit alone now and [wait.]

NANCY. [I've been] told, as part of the whole court thing, that I'll be going to a hospital. Where someone will take care of me for a change.

DAN. I sit by his hospital bed and think about what he might say when he wakes up, if he'd remember it at all. I barely do.

ETHAN. That doesn't make it better.

NANCY. That will be nice. Healthy. Or, I don't know…

DAN. But the doctors, due to the extent of his injuries, they don't think he'll wake up.

ETHAN. *(Lights a cigarette, takes a single drag…)* I just, I wish I could describe the fire to you, [it was…]

NANCY. [It doesn't] matter anyway. No harm [done.]

DAN. [But the thing] I remember most…

ETHAN. *(He lights the lighter, cigarette hanging from his lips…)* Bright.

NANCY. *(She holds out the apple…)* Apple?

DAN. *(Stomps his boot down once, loudly…)* Crush.

Blackout.

THE END

THE ROOSEVELT COUSINS, THOROUGHLY SAUCED

a historical short

By

MICHAEL LEW

To Kristen Harlow and Gregg Mozgala

With thanks to Rehana Mirza

THE ROOSEVELT COUSINS, THOROUGHLY SAUCED premired at Ensemble Studio Theatre (E.S.T.) in the compilation *Thicker Than Water* (February 19-March 10, 2007). The show was produced by Youngblood, E.S.T.'s collective of emerging professional playwrights under 30 (R.J. Tolan and Graeme Gillis, Artistic Directors). The director was Moritz von Stuelpnagel and the cast was as follows:

ELEANOR . . . . Pepper Binkley
FRANKLIN . . . . Gree Mozgala

(1928. Warm Springs, Georgia. Late night. A young **FRANKLIN** *sits in his wheelchair. He is modestly sauced. He pokes at some leftover meatloaf and drinks from a mason jar filled with clear moonshine.* **ELEANOR** *enters. By the way, have you ever heard Eleanor or FDR speak? They talk kind of funny; you should talk like that.)*

ELEANOR. Franklin Delano Roosevelt, I insist you come to bed this instant. Franklin! *(***FRANKLIN*** laughs, then hiccups)* Oh God.

FRANKLIN. *(a deep chuckle)* Uhhhhh ohhhhhhh!

ELEANOR. Oh, Franklin, noooo. Where in God's name are you getting all this alcohol?

FRANKLIN. *(mock pensive)* Hmmmmmmm…

ELEANOR. We are in a state of *Prohibition*, Franklin. Where is this alcohol coming from?

FRANKLIN. It's not alcohol. It's *moonshine!* I mean we're in the middle of *Georgia*. What do you imagine? That all they do in Georgia is sit around eating peaches? Well, they do sit around eating peaches. But in-between peaches they brew this stuff in stills. I got it from a bootlegger, alright? A still-toting, Plantation-owning, mullet-wearing, Southern Confederate Boss Hogg bootlegger.

ELEANOR. Franklin, how do you find it even remotely appropriate to get so… so…

FRANKLIN. Go on. Say it. Say it! Iiiiiiii'm sauced. I'm SAUCED. Schnookered. Tight. Tipsy. Bedrunkened. In-nee-bee-bree-ated. I'm fuckin' fizzaded bomb diggety blasted. Booya.

ELEANOR. Dammit Franklin! You Jacobus Roosevelts are a bunch of incorrigible drunks.

FRANKLIN. Don't you insult my Jacobus Roosevelts. You

Johannes Roosevelts are a lot of joyless, no-good Puritanical Prohibitionists! There, I've said it.

ELEANOR. Don't you insult my Johannes Roosevelts! Uncle Teddy was a Johannes Roosevelt.

FRANKLIN. Phhhh! Teddy. Fuck Teddy. Fat Teddy with his stupid moustache and his size 48 trousers.

ELEANOR. Don't you say that about Uncle Teddy! You loved Teddy!

FRANKLIN. I'm telling the Johannes Roosevelts how you groped me on the polo field at our family reunion.

ELEANOR. Well then I'm telling the Jacobus Roosevelts about that *sex game* you made up where you make me pretend we're second cousins!

FRANKLIN. Well then I'm telling the Johannes Roosevelts how you cry out "Lorena" whenever you climax.

ELEANOR. Well then I'm telling Junior his father's a drunk.

FRANKLIN. Well then I'm telling all our children that they're all a bunch of fucking inbreds!

ELEANOR. Well then I'm telling everyone that you're a fucking cripple! *(she gasps)*

FRANKLIN. *(suddenly morose)* Oh, God. I am a cripple. We're going to stay in this backwater Georgia clinic for the rest of our lives. *(he sobs)* Ugh… I think I just threw up a little in my mouth.

ELEANOR. Franklin. It's late. We're tired. We've both said *things* I'm sure we'd like to forget. Let's start over. I'd kiss you but then again you did just throw up a little in your mouth. Now are you still…

FRANKLIN. What, CRIPPLED?

ELEANOR. No, are you still going to stay out here? Won't you please come to bed?

FRANKLIN. No, Eli. I can't come to bed. Because I CAN'T WALK!

ELEANOR. I didn't mean to call you a cripple; I'm sorry.

FRANKLIN. And what's the deal with this meatloaf? Ya know? This meatloaf fucking sucks.

ELEANOR. It was father's recipe. You know that. It was my father's special meatloaf. He gave me the recipe when I was only ten years old. Then he died like my mother before him and made me an orphan.

FRANKLIN. Yeah well it sucks. Those Johannes Roosevelts don't know *shit* about meatloaf. Those Johannes Roosevelts don't know shit about *shit*loaf! This meatloaf is a meatloaf which will live in infamy!

ELEANOR. If you don't fancy my meatloaf then why don't you WALK TO THE STORE?

FRANKLIN. Oh yeah? I will! I'm gonna get up and walk right now! Watch me. Are you watching? *(he uses his upper body to rise from the wheelchari)* See this? Are you seeing this Eleanor? It's because I'm *strong.* I am ALL ABOUT the hind limb ambulation right now. Uhp… oh no. Uh oh comin' back down *(he falls, the moonshine out of reach)* Pass me the hooch, would you dear?

ELEANOR. Oh, Franklin. You *are* strong. Strong willed, strong-minded. You have great upper body strength. But let's face it – you're not strong enough to beat polio.

FRANKLIN. Lance Armstrong beat polio.

ELEANOR. That was testicular cancer. I mean… Lance Armstrong hasn't been born yet. I mean… who? *(awkward pause)* Alright, pass me the hooch. I'll have one sip. *(she gulps down moonshine)*

FRANKLIN. Yeah so look. I haven't been strong enough to kick polio. YET. But give it another year and… Hey, hey – stop Bogarting the moonshine and pass it.

ELEANOR. I'm feelin kinda *sauced.* Franklin, you know I love you. "Dude, I love you man." But you're not strong enough to beat polio no matter how much money you sink into this clinic. Pass me the hooch. Now listen: it is high time we got you out of Georgia and back into politics.

FRANKLIN. I will. We'll leave the clinic right after I'm fully recovered. I'm almost walking now, aren't I?

ELEANOR. …yesssss…

FRANKLIN. I've been swimming every day haven't I?

ELEANOR. *(her voice echoing from within the moonshine bottle as she sips)* …y…yes…

FRANKLIN. Well then? WELL? Besides, nobody'll vote for me unless they see that I'm fit. Hook me up with the moonshine mami. One more year and *I promise* I'll run for office. Now let's go for a swim.

ELEANOR. I'm feeling kind of *saucy-sauced.* Hooch me the moonshine. I mean pass me the shoeshine. Look. We can't go swimming. You're too drunk for swim. Also: that's not true about people not voting for you just because of your legs. I'd vote for you.

FRANKLIN. Yeah, but women can't vote. Or can they? I dunno. So anyway pop me the hoochshine. Let's go swimming while our vigor is up and our constitution is vital!

ELEANOR. *(sobered)* Ohhhh. Oh maaaan. The Constitution. We're like… totally violating the Constitution. Look, we can't go swimming. It's two in the morning and we're both of us moo-shooed.

FRANKLIN. Don't tell me I'm moo-shooed. I was Secretary of the Navy! I was all like *(bomb sounds)* BSHHH!! Boooshhh! BOOOM! *(plane gunning sounds)* NEEEERM POP POP POP POP POP.

ELEANOR. You have to get to bed so you can pack your bags, return to New York, and run for governor.

FRANKLIN. I was Secretary of the *NAVY*, Popeye! And then we won The Great War and the Germans were all like, "Das is very bad," and we were all like, "Yeah! You pay those reparations, BITCH!" and Woodrow Wilson was all like, "Great job running the Navy, Frankie. You come back to the White House real soon," and then we all danced like *(alarm sound)* OOOP-OOP, OOOP-OOP *(raises the roof).* And… and I was a good dancer then because I had legs that *worked! (he sobs)*

ELEANOR. Ohhhh. Ohhh no. Franklin… Franklin stop

crying. *(Franklin makes a pathetic squeak)* Why you cryin', huh? Why you cryin' Frankie?

FRANKLIN. Because I'm sad.

ELEANOR. Why are you sad?

FRANKLIN. Because my best years are behind me.

ELEANOR. Hey. Hey, who's this? *(deep Teddy Roosevelt voice)* Fuh fuh fuh BULLY. BULLY BULLY! Lookit me and my monocle. Bully!

FRANKLIN. *(laughing)* It's Teddy!

ELEANOR. *(prances about; Teddy voice)* Fuh fuh let's go riding around on our horses with the Rough Riders! Bully! Let's slap my face on Mount Rushmore alongside several presidents who were easily my betters. Bully! Let's make some national parks. BULLY! *(Eleanor voice)* Who's that?

FRANKLIN. IT'S TEDDY!!

ELEANOR. And what would Uncle Teddy do if HE were stuck in Georgia? He wouldn't just sit here shining his monocle. He wouldn't sink all his personal fortunes into a quack clinic for polio victims. Say. Let's *ask Teddy* what he'd do! Uncle Teddy? *(Teddy voice)* Oh Bully! It's Eleanor Roosevelt, my favorite niece. *(Eleanor)* Thank you Teddy I was always so fond of you. *(Teddy)* So what, you wanna get some hotdogs or something? *(Eleanor)* Maybe later. *Franklin* has a question for you.

FRANKLIN. This is silly.

ELEANOR. *(Teddy voice)* Oh Bully! It's Franklin, my favorite nephew. You look like you're all healed up, Champ. Why you oughta run for governor! You don't need that stupid clinic that keeps siphoning off your money… Say, my favorite niece Eleanor says you have a question for me?

FRANKLIN. How can I go back into politics if my legs don't work? How is anyone going to think of me as a strong leader if I'm not strong enough to walk?

ELEANOR. *(Teddy voice)* But you have your wits, Frankie. You have your military experience. Look at that mine defense you invented that protected the Atlantic Seaboard from German U-boats that I read about on the Wikipedia. Why you're the smartest most handsome man I know! Frankie, if you keep dicking around in Georgia speaking softly and holding your big stick, your constituency is going to abandon you!

FRANKLIN. Stop this Eleanor, you don't even sound like him.

ELEANOR. *(Teddy)* Sound like who, Franklin? Iiiii'mmm Teddy. Teddy Roosevelt! Lookit my moustache. Bully! Lookit my big huge belly! Bully! Hey, where's that Taft guy? That pudgy bastard owes me four dollars. Is he stuck in a bathtub again? *(beat; Eleanor)* Oh, alright. Fine. Uncle Teddy go bye now.

FRANKLIN. I can't run for governor. Not like this.

ELEANOR. But I don't LIKE the South, *Franklin*! Nobody educated likes the South.

FRANKLIN. But I don't wanna run for governor. I wanna run for President.

ELEANOR. Governor first.

FRANKLIN. Fuck that. I wanna run for President *now*. I'm gonna be President for like sixteen years.

ELEANOR. That's four terms Franklin.

FRANKLIN. I know how to maths! Damn it all Eleanor why can't you just let a man be? Why can't you just let a man eat his shitty meatloaf and drink his shitty moonshine and be done with it?! *(meek)* Can we go swimming?

ELEANOR. No!

FRANKLIN. Can we play a game?

ELEANOR. What game? The second cousins game? I don't want to play the second cousins game anymore.

FRANKLIN. Can we play the Yankee paraplegic and the seductive Southern hospice nurse?

ELEANOR. How do you play that game?

FRANKLIN. It's easy. You say, *(Southern voice)* "It's time for your sponge bath Mr. Roosevelt." And then I say, "I'm one dirty in-patient," and then you say, *(Southern)* "You Yankees always get so dirty with your skyscrapers and your elevated trains and your speakeasies and your potable water. I bet you don't even fuck your cousins up there." And then I say, "Oh ho… you'd be surprised what we Yankees can do. Let's have a Fireside Chat. *In my pants.*"

ELEANOR. I'm not playing this game. You always weave incest into our sex games and I find it creepy.

FRANKLIN. What if you just pretend to be the hospice nurse and we sorta *see where it goes?* Deal or no deal?

ELEANOR. No deal.

FRANKLIN. Fine. New Deal. You can call me Lorena if you like and we'll engage in some light fingering.

ELEANOR. What about this? What if we pretend that I'm Elise, a French milkmaid from Verdun…

FRANKLIN. Uh huh…

ELEANOR. And then you pretend that you're Stefan, a French soldier…

FRANKLIN. O…kay.

ELEANOR. And you're a tank operator. In your tank here. *(Pats his wheelchair)* See your tank? And it's the Battle of Verdun. The bloodiest battle ever waged. And you're in your tank shelling Germans and I'm hiding here in a cowshed. Suddenly a German soldier creeeeeeeps into the cowshed. What will you do?

FRANKLIN. Ok, ok, so I pull the tank right up to the front of the cowshed. And I say, "Let the girl go!"

ELEANOR. And then what?

FRANKLIN. And then the German sees the tank with the guns pointed right at him and he faints! Faints right in front of the cowshed! And I yell HOP IN and you hop into my tank – hop onto me milkmaid!

ELEANOR. I'm hopping! I'm hopping into your tank! *(She sits on his lap while he rocks back and forth)*

FRANKLIN. And we SQUISH the cowshed! And we SQUISH the German. And we SQUISH all the cows!

ELEANOR. My cows! My cows! You're squishing my cows!

FRANKLIN. And we squish the German. Again. And again. And back. And FORTH. And back. And FORTH.

ELEANOR. Squish him! Oh God squish him squish him.

FRANKLIN. What did you say your name was my little milkmaid?

ELEANOR. I already told you. I'm Elise, a dirty little milkmaid from Verdun.

FRANKLIN. *Elise?* I once had a second cousin named Elise. *She* was a milkmaid from Verdun!

ELEANOR. Franklin!

FRANKLIN. *(she tries to get up but he holds her)* No, no, it's not Franklin. It's your cousin Stefan!

ELEANOR. Dammit Franklin not again.

FRANKLIN. Don't resist me Elise. Don't resist cousin Stefan with his strong French upper body strength.

ELEANOR. *(laughing, whining)* Fraaaankliiiiin. Stoooop!

FRANKLIN. Okay. *(she snuggles into him)* Oof. All that rocking. My stomach hurts. *(beat)* I'm so miserable.

ELEANOR. What?

FRANKLIN. This wheelchair and this disease and this whole fucking thing. You didn't sign up to marry an invalid. Back before the polio I wouldn't have let indigestion or your protests halt our sex play.

ELEANOR. Oh but sweetums. It's not the polio it's all the hard drinking. Don't you remember our wedding? Remember how drunk we got and how you carried me piggyback across the polo field? How you passed out by a pile of horseshit and dropped me on my wedding day and gave me a concussion?

FRANKLIN. Ohhhh yeaaaahhh. Hey remember how the preacher said "If anyone has any reason why these two *cousins* shouldn't marry…" and then he just sat there glaring at us?

ELEANOR. How the ushers said, "Are you with the bride's side or the groom's?" with that knowing chuckle?

FRANKLIN. I remember. *(beat)* Hey Eli?

ELEANOR. Mmm?

FRANKLIN. You know I'll run for governor don't you?

ELEANOR. I know.

FRANKLIN. And then I'll run for president! I'm going to be president for like seventeen years.

ELEANOR. Try being president for four years first. Try being governor first.

FRANKLIN. But I will be president. Because I was a senator. And I ran the Navy.

ELEANOR. You were all like *(plane sounds)* Neeeeeeerm-mmm *(gun sounds)* Pupp-pah-pupp-pa-pah.

FRANKLIN. Yeah I was all like that. So they'll vote for me bad legs and all. And when I run for President, *(Howard Dean voice)* not only are we going to New Hampshire… we're going to South Carolina and Oklahoma and Arizona, and North Dakota and New Mexico, and we're going to California and Texas and New York… and we're going to South Dakota. And Oregon. And Washington and Michigan and then we're going to Washington DC to take back the White House. Byaaaaaaaah!

ELEANOR. *(beat)* That moonshine was good. Fuck Prohibition!

FRANKLIN. Fuck it indeed, my dear. Fuck Prohibition indeed.

ELEANOR. We violated the Constitution today. Fuckin'… take that, *democracy.*

FRANKLIN. Yes, democracy. Take it right in the ear. Let's go to bed, Eli. Shall I wheel you to bed?

ELEANOR. No, let's stand. Do you want to try walking?

(She helps **FRANKLIN** *to stand. Propped up by* **ELEANOR**, **FRANKLIN** *walks gingerly out of the room with her.)*

END OF PLAY

EVERY MAN

By

MICHAEL NIEDERMAN

CHARACTERS

SAVANNAH - A fifteen year old girl, awkward and used to being out of place. She speaks with her own language at times, and is not unfamiliar with living in a world of her own design. She is just starting to understand this is the very reason why she is as large an outcast as she is.

WENDY - Savannah's mother, in her early thirties. She, long ago, has given up any notion of her girlhood dreams, and for a very good reason, and she looks on Savannah's constant wonder and naiveté with a mixture of jealousy and trepidation.

PETER - Ageless. Magical. Beautiful. Selfish. Completely without regard for the consequences of his actions.

(*A backyard. Night.*)

(**SAVANNAH** *[15] sits in her backyard. She looks up at the stars.*)

SAVANNAH. Look! That one's my star. The second star to the right. My mother gave it to me when I was just a little girl. It doesn't have a name. You can't name stars, silly. I'm sure they've got their own names. In star languages that we can't even understand. Like, one star might say to another star-

(*she says something in "Star Language". It's probably high and piercing, but who knows?*)

And then the other star would reply

(*again, a phrase in "Star Language"*)

And us on earth would have no idea what they're saying. Probably something about the price of neon gas or how they haven't seen any comets in 71 years.

(*She talks in "Star Language" again, this time to the sky.*)

SAVANNAH. I think I said hello. But you can never be too sure.

(**WENDY** *[31] yells from inside the house.*)

WENDY (O.S.) Savannah! Savannah! It's time to come inside!

SAVANNAH. In a minute, Mom.

WENDY (O.S.) It's time for bed!

SAVANNAH. In a minute!

(**WENDY** *sticks her head out the window.*)

WENDY. Did you did your homework?

SAVANNAH. Yes, mom.

WENDY. I can check your books.

SAVANNAH. Check my books. I don't care.

WENDY. I will.

SAVANNAH. Go ahead.

(WENDY *sticks her head back inside.*)

WENDY (O.S.) Savannah!

SAVANNAH. What?

WENDY (O.S.) Where is your chemistry homework?

SAVANNAH. There wasn't any?

WENDY. *(sticking her head back out.)* It's not too late to call your teacher.

SAVANNAH. Chemistry isn't until 6th period. I'll do it at lunch.

WENDY. *(joining her daughter outside)* I don't like you doing things at the last minute.

SAVANNAH. Mom! Can't you just – look at the stars with me. For a bit.

WENDY. Okay. But no talking to the stars. It gives me a headache.

(*The two of them sit in silence.*)

SAVANNAH. Mom?

WENDY. Yeah, honey?

SAVANNAH. Do you think I'm pretty?

WENDY. Of course you are.

SAVANNAH. Then how come none of the boys like me?

WENDY. Well, you're still young. Give it time.

SAVANNAH. I've had nothing but time. I see the how the boys look at the other girls, the one's that have filled out more than I have. No one looks at me the same way.

WENDY. It's all in your head.

SAVANNAH. I'm not stupid, Mom. They don't look at me in the eyes. Or anywhere else.

WENDY. I think you're spending too much time looking at boys, and not enough at your books.

SAVANNAH. I try to be nice and different and cool. Do you think that it's because I try to talk to the stars?

(She says something again in "Star Language." Her mother hushes her.)

WENDY. Perhaps.

SAVANNAH. They don't look at me with want. I want to be wanted.

WENDY. Well, we all enjoy attention.

SAVANNAH. Mom, how old where you when you first got a boyfriend?

WENDY. Time for bed.

SAVANNAH. Mom.

WENDY. Well, I – I was older than you, that's for sure.

SAVANNAH. I'm fifteen.

WENDY. I know how old you are. Do we have to do this now?

SAVANNAH. Do what?

WENDY. The whole "facts of life" talk. You know, boys only want one thing.

SAVANNAH. Which one thing?

WENDY. You don't know?

SAVANNAH. Know what?

WENDY. Savannah, don't make me say it.

SAVANNAH. Yes, Mom. I know. We have HBO. I know all about sex.

WENDY. Well, that's just wonderful. And now you're depressed that you're not getting any. You're not getting any, are you?

SAVANNAH. I guess not.

WENDY. You guess? What are they teaching you kids in school?

SAVANNAH. I'm still a virgin!

WENDY. That's nice.

SAVANNAH. And I don't want to have sex. Yet.

WENDY. You've made your mother very proud.

SAVANNAH. But a boyfriend would be nice. I go to school every day and no one talks to me. I feel like no one knows me.

WENDY. I know you. And I know you've got to go to bed.

SAVANNAH. Mom – ?

WENDY. And no one's going to talk to you tomorrow because you're going to spend lunch alone in the library doing the chemistry homework that you should have done tonight instead of making me worry that you're out getting pregnant. I'm going inside.

(**WENDY** *goes inside.*)

SAVANNAH. I could be cool. If I tried hard enough. I could get people to like me. If I tried hard enough. I could say the right things at all the right times and everybody would look up to me and then I would be cool. And all the boys would like me.

(**PETER** *enters. He's a young man, incredibly handsome, and magical.* **SAVANNAH** *falls under his spell.*)

PETER. Hey. How you doing?

SAVANNAH. Hi. Do I know you?

PETER. No. I'm new. My name's Peter.

SAVANNAH. I've got to go inside.

PETER. It's not even eleven.

SAVANNAH. I've got school tomorrow.

PETER. You go to school too? Me too. I go to school all the time.

SAVANNAH. Of course I go to school. I'm only fifteen.

PETER. Only fifteen? There is no only fifteen. Fifteen is the cusp of the rest of your life. I'm Peter.

SAVANNAH. I'm Savannah.

PETER. Savannah. Such a nice name.

SAVANNAH. Oh, I don't like it. Makes me sound like an old lady.

PETER. You don't look like an old lady to me. You look... You look fifteen. I like fifteen. It's a cusp. I like cusps.

SAVANNAH. Cusps?

PETER. It means the edge. Just after something, but right before something else. That's where you are, Savannah. You're on the cusp.

SAVANNAH. My birthday's not for another eight months.

PETER. I wasn't talking about chronological age. Though I so do love fifteen.

SAVANNAH. How old did you say you were again?

PETER. I didn't.

SAVANNAH. Well, how old are you?

PETER. Eighteen?

SAVANNAH. So you're a senior?

PETER. Yeah, I'm a senior.

SAVANNAH. Do you know where you're going to college yet? Because I'm just starting that whole process. My mom says I need to get my grades up and do some more extra curricular activities if I want to go anywhere good, but I don't know if I want to go to college yet. I might work summers and save for a trip to Europe for a year and then worry about the rest of my life. I mean, what is college, anyway, but a place where you study the work of a bunch of dead straight white guys who –

PETER. Shhhh. You talk too much.

(Silence. She fiddles with the hem of her skirt.)

PETER. That's why you can't get a boyfriend.

SAVANNAH. I do that sometimes when I get nervous.

PETER. You need to listen more.

(Silence.)

SAVANNAH. Hey, you want to hear me talk to a star?

PETER. No. I want to see you without your shirt on.

SAVANNAH. What?

PETER. You've been wanting to ever since I sat down. Right?

SAVANNAH. No!

PETER. Then why can't you stop fiddling with the hem of
your skirt and the neck of you blouse?

SAVANNAH. Because it's hot. And you're making me nervous. The way you're staring at me.

PETER. I thought that's what you wanted. Boys to stare at
you. Instead of passing you by as they look for the girls
who put out. Really know you. Savannah, I think I
know you.

SAVANNAH. You just met me.

PETER. I know that no one understands you, and it tears
you up inside. That you've got hopes and dreams
bigger than this town, of seaside resorts and continental breakfasts with tall men whose hair falls into their
eyes.

SAVANNAH. What's a continental breakfast?

PETER. It's just like a regular one, except with a fruit plate.
Forget about breakfast. What do you want to do?

SAVANNAH. I don't know. My mom thinks I should go to
college and become a doctor or lawyer or –

PETER. I'm not talking about what your mother wants.

SAVANNAH. I don't know what I want.

PETER. I'd like to kiss you. If that's okay.

SAVANNAH. I guess so. A quick one. I've got to go inside
soon.

PETER. Well, we can't keep Mother waiting.

(*They kiss.* **SAVANNAH** *starts to swoon into his arms, but
stops herself at the last moment.*)

PETER. How did that feel?

SAVANNAH. Okay, I guess.

PETER. Did it make you feel warm inside, in your stomach?
So delightfully warm, yet itchy, and all you can think to
do is reach down scratch?

SAVANNAH. Do you want me to take off my shirt?

PETER. Savannah, I thought you'd never ask.

(*She starts to unbutton her shirt.*)

(WENDY enters.)

WENDY. Savannah. It's time to go inside.

PETER. Just one minute, Mom.

WENDY. Now.

(SAVANNAH does.)

WENDY. I think you should go now, too.

PETER. Where should I go to?

WENDY. Wherever people like you come from.

PETER. I've always been here. Don't you remember me?

WENDY. Should I?

PETER. I'd feel real blue if you didn't remember me.

WENDY. I've known men like you. Men who think they can prey on naive girls like my daughter.

PETER. She's not that naive. She's young, sure, but there's a real fire inside that one, just waiting to burn.

(WENDY slaps him.)

WENDY. I told you never to talk like that again.

PETER. You do remember me. I thought your memory was fading with old age, Wendy.

WENDY. I'm not that old. How come you look the same?

PETER. I'll always look like this. This is what I am.

WENDY. You should go now. And never come back.

PETER. Don't you want to talk?

WENDY. I've got nothing to say to you.

PETER. I thought we spent good times together.

WENDY. You don't have to live with the regret. You never had to.

PETER. You don't know what I live with.

(She starts to go inside.)

PETER. Wendy, I've missed you.

WENDY. She's just a child.

PETER. So were you.

WENDY. That was a long time ago.

PETER. I remember we used to meet in the woods behind your house. We'd lie under a tree all afternoon and you'd tell me stories of what your life would be like.

WENDY. No one ever listened to me back then.

PETER. How many listen to you now?

WENDY. I don't think you should come around here anymore.

PETER. One last dance.

WENDY. No. Not that.

PETER. Please. Just one. And then I'll go.

(He snaps his fingers. A slow, sad torch song plays. Maybe "Lady Stardust" by David Bowie.)

(He holds his hands out for **WENDY.** *She hesitates for a moment, then collapses in his arms. They dance.)*

WENDY. God, I forgot how good this felt.

PETER. I never meant to hurt you. You or anyone close to you.

WENDY. I just missed you so much.

PETER. But you moved on. It happens. I'm used to it now.

WENDY. Your arms. I feel so safe in your arms.

PETER. I could stay here. I could keep you safe.

WENDY. Ever since I knew you I've been running from you. Running from how safe I feel in your arms.

PETER. The three of us could be a family. You and me and Savannah. I could make you all happy.

WENDY. Happy.

PETER. Happy. Me and all my girls. And if Savannah were to have a daughter, we'll be happier still.

(She stays in his arms for a moment. She then pushes him away. The music stops.)

WENDY. No! No, you are not going to do this to me again.

PETER. Wendy, come on. Remember how you loved me? Don't you want Savannah to have that love?

WENDY. You keep away from me. And you keep away from my daughter.

PETER. But there are so many things I could teach her.

WENDY. Life will happen to her no matter what. You will not make her rush. My daughter won't live with the same regret I've had.

PETER. I'll always be a part of you.

WENDY. That part of me's been dead for a long time.

PETER. Do you really want me to go?

(**WENDY** *says nothing.* **PETER** *goes to leave.*)

WENDY. Peter?

PETER. Yes, Wendy?

WENDY. Say hello to the stars for me.

PETER. You're all we ever talk about.

(**PETER** *leaves.*)

(**WENDY** *looks up at the sky. The music swells again.* **WENDY** *says something in "Star Language".*)

(*Black out.*)

THE GOOD BOOK

By

TIFFANY ANTONE

THE GOOD BOOK was first produced by UCLA and Latino Theater Company in June 2007 as part of the Thirty Second Annual Samuel French, Inc Off Off Broadway Short Play Festival. The production was directed by Jose Luis Valenzuela, with the following cast:

ROBERT. . . . . Robert Beltran
LUCINDA. . . . . Evelina Fernández
MARIELLA. . . . . Camden Gonzales

ABOUT THE AUTHOR

Tiffany Antone is currently completing her MFA degree in Playwriting at UCLA where she has received the James Pendelton Foundation Prize, the Hal Kanter Award in Comedy Writing, Dini Ostrov Stage Spirit Award in Playwriting, the Steve Lawrence and Eydie Gorme Scholarship, and the Florence Theil Herrscher Award. Her Plays have been read and performed in Los angeles, New York and she soon travels to Minneapolis with her play *In the Company of Jane Doe* (A Princess Grace semi-finalist for 2006) as one of three selected to particepate in this years "New Plays on Campus" series at The Playwrights' Center. Other plays include *Ham Brown's House, Little Phoenix, Stalled, My Pet George,* and *From the Rubble.*

CHARACTERS

ROBERT – Latino, in his 40's
LUCINDA – Latina, ageless
MARIELLA – Latina, 13

PLACE

A home

TIME

Now

COSTUMES

ROBERT – Pajamas
LUCINDA – Flowing white nightgown
MARIELLA – Pajamas, a robe

PROPERTY LIST

Small Clock
Lamp
Sheets (on bed, plus 1 extra set)
Very Large Scrap Book
Decorative Paper Bag containing:
1 Bottle of Wine, 2 Wine Glasses
1 Pink Boa
1 Envelope Marked "Mariella"

(A home. A bedroom of moderate means exists up right. A queen-size bed dressed in blue rests against the SL wall, a large picture window on the upstage wall lets in a full moon, and a weathered rocking chair sits up right. From the bedroom a hallway leads to another, smaller, bedroom, dressed for a young girl. A bathroom door is visible from the hallway. When opened, it is possible to see the bathroom mirror and sink.

**It is also possible, if a smaller space is used, to utilize one bedroom, and simply change the dressings when Robert runs to Mariella's room. The bathroom works perfectly fine as a door leading offstage.*

At rise, the moonlight is shining into the bedroom in all her glory. A light glows from beneath the bathroom door. There is a flush and **ROBERT**, *40, opens the bathroom door drying his hands. He is wearing pajamas. He enters the bedroom, sits down on the bed. A woman's pale arms come from beneath the sheets and wrap around his chest. It is* **LUCINDA**, *his wife. She is dressed in a long white nightgown, and her long brown hair frames her beautiful face.)*

ROBERT. Did I wake you?

LUCINDA. I couldn't sleep anyway.

ROBERT. I'm sorry. I shouldn't have flushed. It always wakes you.

LUCINDA. Then why do you do it?

ROBERT. When I don't flush, Mariella gets up in the morning and I can hear her yelling all the way up here –

LUCINDA. What do you expect. She's a teenager.

ROBERT. Not yet, she isn't!

LUCINDA. It's April 12th.

ROBERT. Tomorrow.

LUCINDA. Look at the clock.

(He does.)

ROBERT. Oh my God.

LUCINDA. 12:01.

ROBERT. On the nose.

LUCINDA. It's a girl –

ROBERT. A baby Lucy –

LUCINDA. She has your eyes.

ROBERT. And your big mouth –

LUCINDA. Hey.

ROBERT. I'm just joking.

(Beat)

I always loved your mouth.

(He brushes her hair from her face.)

LUCINDA. You're a papa.

ROBERT. Two of you to love.

LUCINDA. To hold.

ROBERT. To worry about.

LUCINDA. To take care of.

(There is a long pause.)

ROBERT. Can she really be thirteen already?

LUCINDA. Yes.

ROBERT. God, we're getting old.

LUCINDA. Speak for yourself!

ROBERT. *(Sigh)* I found a gray hair.

LUCINDA. I don't believe you.

ROBERT. Believe it. I found it before I went to bed. Mariella asked me if she can invite a boy to her party. I felt a sharp pain in my head and my vision got cloudy, I ran to the bathroom and the son of a bitch was right there, laughing at me in the mirror.

LUCINDA. Pobrecito.

ROBERT. I pulled him out, flushed him down the toilet, but not before he flipped me the bird, told me he was calling all his friends, first chance he gets. I'm going to be silver by morning, I just know it.

LUCINDA. *(laughing gently)* So what did you tell her?

ROBERT. Huh?

LUCINDA. About the boy?

ROBERT. I said okay. I was in shock. My daughter asks me if she can invite her boyfriend to our house, I find my first gray hair, I'm lucky I could speak at all.

LUCINDA. She's getting older, it's only natural she's going to be curious about boys.

(He stands up, uncomfortable.)

ROBERT. Oh, don't talk to me about that. I can't think about my little girl going out with some, some –

LUCINDA. She's not a little girl anymore –

ROBERT. Yes she is, she's my little girl. My little mockingbird. She'll always be my little –

LUCINDA. She's a woman.

ROBERT. What? No she isn't – she's just thirteen –

LUCINDA. She's a woman tonight.

*(**ROBERT** stares at her.)*

ROBERT. You mean –

LUCINDA. Yes.

(There is a sudden yell from down the hall, in Mariella's room.)

MARIELLA. Papa!

LUCINDA. She's got her period.

*(**ROBERT** grabs his head.)*

ROBERT. Oh my god! Another gray hair!

(He turns to her)

Lucinda, look, I feel it –

*(But **LUCINDA** has disappeared.)*

MARIELLA. Papa! Bring the book!

(**ROBERT** *looks around himself, realizes he is alone.*)

ROBERT. Yes, mija, I'm coming.

(*He grabs a giant scrap book from the shelf, and runs down the hall. He tries to open the door, but* **MARIELLA,** *13 years and 2 minutes old, is on the other side, holding it closed. She has her mother's long brown hair, and bright yearning eyes. She wears pajamas, and might have braces.*)

ROBERT. Ai, Mariella, open the door.

MARIELLA. No, go away.

ROBERT. But you just called for me –

MARIELLA. I changed my mind.

ROBERT. Why? What's going on?

MARIELLA. I'm, I think I'm dying papa.

ROBERT. No, mija, it's just your period.

(**MARIELLA** *claps her hands to her ears and screams. Robert opens the door.*)

ROBERT. Mariella- shhh.

MARIELLA. Gross! Gross! Gross!!!!

ROBERT. What are you yelling for? It's a beautiful thing my darling! You are becoming a woman, una mujer –

MARIELLA. No!

ROBERT. No?

MARIELLA. No!

ROBERT. Okay.

(**MARIELLA** *looks at him, confused.*)

MARIELLA. Okay?

ROBERT. Sure. You said no, so I guess that means no. Sounds good to me. I don't want you growing up. I want to keep you little and pink and wearing ribbons to school –

MARIELLA. *(groaning)* Dad!

ROBERT. What?

MARIELLA. I haven't worn ribbons is ages!

ROBERT. Ah, you're right. What was I thinking?

(She looks at him warily.)

MARIELLA. Did you bring it?

ROBERT. Si, I got it right here. Are you okay?

MARIELLA. I feel a little sick.

ROBERT. Well, let's see what your mama has to say, no?

(MARIELLA nods.)

ROBERT. Can I turn on the light?

(MARIELLA nods. He flips on the bedside lamp.)

ROBERT. That's better.

(He starts to sit on the bed, MARIELLA stops him.)

MARIELLA. Dad –

ROBERT. Oh, right. Of course. I'll just sit over here, okay?

MARIELLA. Okay. God.

(He sits on the floor, opens the book and starts flipping the pages.)

ROBERT. Let's see... I know it's going to be here... I hope it's here –

MARIELLA. Me too –

ROBERT. I just don't know what to look under –

MARIELLA. How about "P"?

ROBERT. What? Oh, right, for "Panic."

(He laughs at his joke)

Okay. Calmate. P, P... Here we are – under the sink.

MARIELLA. What?

ROBERT. She says to look under the sink, she left some, things, for you there. And directions. Okay, I'll go get them for you –

(He starts to get up.)

MARIELLA. No, Dad – I'll get it.

ROBERT. Oh, good. I mean, okay. If you want to.

MARIELLA. I do.

ROBERT. Okay.

(She clears her throat expectantly.)

ROBERT. Oh! Right, I think there's some other stuff here I'm supposed to read –

(He starts studying the book more closely, so as to provide **MARIELLA** *an opportunity to scoot past him into the hallway. She grabs her robe on her way to the bathroom. She makes it past him and closes the door behind her.* **ROBERT** *almost passes out from the stress.)*

ROBERT. Ay, dios mio. What a night!

MARIELLA. *(From the bathroom)* Oh, GROSS!

ROBERT. You alright mija?

MARIELLA. *(From the bathroom)* Yes.

*(***LUCINDA*** is standing over him. He jumps in surprise.)*

ROBERT. Oh, Lucinda, thank God you're here! I can't handle this. Did you see the look on her face? She was mortified!

LUCINDA. She'll be fine.

ROBERT. How? How will she be fine? I'm a complete idiota right now. I can't even see straight!

LUCINDA. She'll be fine. It's you I'm worried about.

ROBERT. Me?

LUCINDA. You look like you've seen a ghost.

ROBERT. *(Serious)* That's not funny.

LUCINDA. It was kind of funny.

ROBERT. This is serious. What am I supposed to do now?

LUCINDA. Didn't you look under the sink?

ROBERT. She's doing that.

LUCINDA. And what are you doing?

ROBERT. I'm trying to get my breath back, what do you think?

LUCINDA. What good is that thing if you don't read it?

(She picks up the book and reads.)

LUCINDA. "Robert, my brave and wonderful man, I am sure you will be missing me very much on this day –"

ROBERT. You can say that again.

LUCINDA. *(Continuing)* "– This is the most important day in a woman's life, because it is the day in which the gift of life shines brightest for her. It is the day when the moon comes into her womb and blesses her with the light of the universe, and she must never forget that this is the mark of the goddess. You must make her feel special, that she has been welcomed into the arms of all her ancestors, as the beautiful young woman she has become."

ROBERT. That's a lot of pressure.

LUCINDA. You can do it. I put something in the hall closet to help you.

ROBERT. What?

LUCINDA. Go look.

*(**ROBERT** gets up, goes to the hall closet.)*

ROBERT. I don't see anything.

LUCINDA. In the back –

ROBERT. Mothballs?

LUCINDA. No.

ROBERT. What have we here?

*(He removes a large paper bag that has been carefully tied closed. He opens the bag, looks inside, shakes his head and closes it. He heads back to the bedroom but not before taking some fresh sheets from the linen closet. **ROBERT** and **LUCINDA** proceed to make the bed together under the following dialogue.)*

ROBERT. You have one hell of a sense of humor.

LUCINDA. I know.

ROBERT. We can never move you know. You've got things hidden all over this house, I would never be able to find it all –

LUCINDA. Do you want to move?

ROBERT. (*Sincerely*) No.

LUCINDA. Good. But if you ever did, you could always just read the whole book and relocate things in the new house –

ROBERT. No. It wouldn't be the same. This way, it's like a treasure hunt –

LUCINDA. A game.

ROBERT. A good one.

(*Beat*)

Besides. I could never read that whole thing. It's an encyclopedia. Sometimes, I wonder how you managed to do it all –

LUCINDA. I was determined.

ROBERT. You thought of everything –

LUCINDA. I'm a mother –

ROBERT. But still...

LUCINDA. I knew you might need it –

ROBERT. Psh, might? It's like our bible. Remember when she was a baby and you went out with your girlfriends for the first time since we had her?

LUCINDA. How could I forget?

ROBERT. It was the first time I had been alone with her. She was this helpless little thing...

LUCINDA. Que preciosa – I knew you would be fine.

ROBERT. She fell asleep on her ear –

LUCINDA. (*Laughing*) Me acuerdo – you called me so upset, "I broke her. I broke our daughter's ear!"

ROBERT. She woke up and it was folded over, stuck to her head like, an elf. I thought for sure you would be leaving me for someone better suited –

LUCINDA. I came home early –

ROBERT. You just smiled and pulled it back –

LUCINDA. It was just stuck to her cheek –

ROBERT. And everything was back to normal. She was perfect. You always knew what to do.

LUCINDA. You'll be fine Roberto, both of you.

(The bed is made, **ROBERT** *and* **LUCINDA** *lift the blanket up together, but when it comes down on the bed,* **LUCINDA** *is gone and* **MARIELLA** *stands in the doorway.)*

MARIELLA. Who were you talking to?

ROBERT. No one. Your mother. I'm a little nervous. Everything all right?

MARIELLA. Yes. You changed the sheets?

ROBERT. Yes.

MARIELLA. How embarrassing!

ROBERT. No, mija, you should not be embarrassed. Your mother would not want you to feel bad. She wants you to feel like a... A Goddess –

MARIELLA. Dad...

ROBERT. No, little woman, listen to me. This is a very special day! Come here, see.

(He shows her the bag)

ROBERT. She left me something too!

MARIELLA. What is it?

ROBERT. A surprise. Ven aqui, we'll look inside together.

(Together they look in the bag. **ROBERT** *has already done this, but* **MARIELLA,** *seeing inside for the first time lets out a big laugh.)*

ROBERT. Your mother, she was a joker, no?

(He removes a pink boa, and a bottle of red wine. **MARIELLA** *reacts to each item with humor, turning to seriousness when he also removes an envelope addressed to Mariella.)*

ROBERT. Hmm, looks like she wrote something down just for you.

(He offers her the letter, but she grabs the boa instead.)

MARIELLA. What does the book say about this?

(**ROBERT** *puts the letter down, picks up the book.*)

ROBERT. Let's see...

(*reading*)

"Something fluffy for my baby, and a glass of wine for my mujercita. Sit in a hot bath mija and listen to the waves. You can hear your tia and me laughing at the follies of men. (Sorry Robert) You have joined us now Mariella. I love you mi preciosa."

(*There is a moment of silence.*)

MARIELLA. I can have a glass of wine?

ROBERT. Looks like it. Should I get the corkscrew?

MARIELLA. Okay.

(**ROBERT** *gets up, walks into the hallway and offstage presumably to the kitchen, returning with a corkscrew and two glasses. While he is gone,* **MARIELLA** *picks up the envelope and smells it, caressing it lovingly, but she does not open it.* **ROBERT** *returns and sets to opening the bottle.*)

ROBERT. She picked a good wine. I wonder how many bottles of this she has hidden around here?

MARIELLA. In case of emergency?

ROBERT. This is a celebration!

MARIELLA. Dad –

ROBERT. Mariella.

(*Beat.*)

MARIELLA. This boa is so soft.

ROBERT. You look like a flamingo!

MARIELLA. Dad! Come on!

ROBERT. Where are we going?

MARIELLA. Dad, you're so corny.

ROBERT. Mande? You think I'm a corn?

MARIELLA. No, corny –

ROBERT. Oh, si, well I am.

(He hands her a glass of wine.)

ROBERT. To you, my little angel woman.

(He toasts her, they each take a drink of the wine.)

MARIELLA. We should toast to mama too.

ROBERT. Yes. Tu mama, Lucinda.

MARIELLA. The most beautiful angel of them all.

ROBERT. Mi amor.

(They clink glasses again and drink. There is a moment of reflection.)

MARIELLA. Papa, do you miss her?

ROBERT. Everyday. Do you?

MARIELLA. All the time.

*(**MARIELLA** still holds the envelope.)*

ROBERT. How are you feeling?

MARIELLA. Fine. Not so freaked out. I think maybe I'll take a bath. Like she said.

ROBERT. Do you need bubbles?

MARIELLA. I can do it.

ROBERT. Oh. Okay. I can leave then –

MARIELLA. Do you think she'd be proud of me?

ROBERT. Oh, mija, your mother is very proud. She watches over you always, and you make her so very happy and proud because of what a wonderful and beautiful young woman you are becoming.

MARIELLA. Thanks dad.

ROBERT. I mean it.

*(**MARIELLA** picks up the envelope and her glass of wine and heads to the bathroom. She closes the door behind her. **ROBERT** turns to **LUCINDA**.*

She smiles down on him.)

ROBERT. What is in the envelope?

LUCINDA. My grandmother's necklace.

ROBERT. Oh wow.

LUCINDA. It's a woman's necklace.

ROBERT. *(Soft)* She's going to be okay, no?

LUCINDA. She's going to be perfect.

    (A bright light glows from beneath the door as **MARIELLA** *opens the envelope and accepts her birthright.)*

THE END

OFF-OFF-BROADWAY FESTIVAL PLAYS

TWENTY-SECOND SERIES

Brothers   This Is How It Is   Because I Wanted to Say Tremulous   The Last Dance   For Tiger Lilies Out of Season   The Most Perfect Day

TWENTY-THIRD SERIES

The Way to Miami   Harriet Tubman Visits a Therapist   Meridan, Mississippi   Studio Portrait   It's Okay, Honey   Francis Brick Needs No Introduction

TWENTY-FOURTH SERIES

The Last Cigarette   Flight of Fancy   Physical Therapy   Nothing in the World Like It   The Price You Pay   Pearls Ophelia   A Significant Betrayal

TWENTY-FIFTH SERIES

Strawberry Fields   Sin Inch Adjustable   Evening Education   Hot Rot   A Pink Cadillac Nightmare   East of the Sun and West of the Moon

TWENTY-SIXTH SERIES

Tickets, Please!   Someplace Warm   The Test   A Closer Look   A Peace Replaced   Three Tables

TWENTY-SEVENTH SERIES

Born to Be Blue   The Parrot   Flights   A Doctor's Visit   Three Questions   The Devil's Parole

TWENTY-EIGHTH SERIES

Along for the Ride   A Low-Lying Fog   Blueberry Waltz   The Ferry   Leaving Tangier   Quick & Dirty (A Subway Fantasy)

TWENTY-NINTH SERIES

All in Little Pieces   The Casseroles of Far Rockaway   Feet of Clay   The King and the Condemned   My Wife's Coat   The Theodore Roosevelt Rotunda

THIRTIETH SERIES

Defacing Michael Jackson   The Ex   Kerry and Angie   Outside the Box   Picture Perfect   The Sweet Room

THIRTY-FIRST SERIES

Le Supermarché   Libretto   Play #3   Sick   Pischer   Relationtrip

THIRTY-SECOND SERIES

Opening   Circuit Breakers   Bright. Apple. Crush   The Roosevelt Cousins, Thoroughly Sauced   Every Man   The Good Book

SAMUELFRENCH.COM